I wish you friendships
happiness every day.
Jean E. Cutler

Apples, Oranges, Beans and Peas, Dancing Doggies and Singing Bees

Ben the Storyteller

by

Jean E. Cutler

DORRANCE PUBLISHING CO
EST. 1920
PITTSBURGH, PENNSYLVANIA 15238

Dorrance Publishing Co
585 Alpha Drive, Suite 103
Pittsburgh, PA 15238
Visit our website at *www.dorrancebookstore.com*

ISBN: 978-1-4809-4639-2
eISBN: 978-1-4809-4616-3

ACKNOWLEDGEMENTS

In appreciation of my dear mother, Min Cutler, who raised me with a smile on her face, kindness in her eyes, and the "Golden Rule" in her heart. She helped me, from afar, to write my play. Years later, I felt her presence help me create this book containing my play. So, this book was born with love, from my mom.

With acknowledgement and love to:

My son Stephen Jay Schwartz and daughter-in-law Ryen Schwartz; my grandsons, Benjamin and Noah Schwartz; my daughter, Rennie Morian; my son-in-law Frank Morian, and their family members; my sister, Helen Abraham and brother-in-law, Fred Schreiner, and their families; my brother Ed Cutler, sister-in-law Renee Cutler, and their family members; my brother, Allan Cutler, and his family; and my dear mate and special helper, Don Barbaree, and his family.

SPECIAL THANKS to my grandsons, Ben and Noah Schwartz, for allowing me to use their youthful pictures to portray Ben and Noah in this book.

For technical support, thanks to: IMITAC A.C. and Ri Anderson, Photoshop specialist.

ILLUSTRATIONS CREATED, DRAWN, AND COLORED
BY
DON BARBAREE AND JEAN CUTLER

Thank you to all the wonderful cast members on the enclosed DVD

JEAN CUTLER, AUTHOR

BEN: Hi Noah. Hey, Bro what's the matter? You mad about something?

NOAH: Sure I am. Mommy and Dad say I can't play 'til I eat all my vegetables and fruit, too. YUCK! I don't like them. I just like chocolate milk and corn dogs.

BEN: Oh come on, Noah. Fruits and vegetables are healthy. You want to grow strong, don't you? Hey, I'll tell you a great story about a family of fruits and vegetables. Do you want me to tell you the story?

NOAH: Oh, sure. A fruits and vegetables family. Do they sing and dance too? Oh brother.

BEN: Believe me, kid. You'll like it.

NOAH: Okay, Ben. Go ahead. You always tell me good stories.

BEN: Get comfortable, then. The name of the story is "APPLES, ORANGES, BEANS AND PEAS, DANCING DOGGIES AND SINGING BEES." It takes place in an orchard, sort of like this yard, where apples and oranges grow on trees.

NOAH: "APPLES, ORANGES, BEANS AND PEAS, DANCING DOGGIES AND SINGING BEES" WHOA! That's a good one!

"And now the play begins"

Apples, Oranges, Beans and Peas, Dancing Doggies and Singing Bees

APPLES, ORANGES, BEANS AND PEAS, DANCING DOGGIES AND SINGING BEES

EXTERIOR SCENE: BEAUTIFUL ORCHARD   DAY

A group of eight apples and oranges are baking pies, washing clothes, and preparing for the annual Spring Festival. ORA, a young, female orange, and RIPPLEY, a young, male apple, skip up to APPLE-ACIA, RIPPLEY'S mother. APPLE-ACIA is a delicious, red apple.

RIPPLEY

Can we help with the pies, Mom?

APPLE-ACIA

Go along, go along, you can join in the song when the doggies and bees come to play!

JONATHAN APPLESEED

I'm so happy today. It's a great day for a party.

VENCIA

Yes it is. You're certainly right. Our annual festival is going to be bright.

APPLE-ACIA breaks into song.

Song #1

I'm such a happy apple,

I'm such a happy apple.

Today's a beautiful day.

I've never been so excited,

I'm simply delighted.

It's a glorious day, in May.

This orchard smells delicious,

It's pretty and nutritious.

Soon our friends will be here.

I've never been so excited,

I'm simply delighted.

Listen. Listen.

I think I hear their cheer!

Their friends, the DOGGIES, enter singing and cheering. The two groups join together, dancing around the Maypole. RIPPLEY and ORA join along, singing, dancing, and having fun.

SONG #1-CONTINUED

We're celebrating springtime,

When the sun comes shining through.

We just blossom, we're so pretty and alive.

And the sky is so blue.

APPLE-ACIA

The sun is shining. It's a beautiful spring day.

I can't wait 'til the festivities get under way.

SWEET APPLE

>Honey darlings, we are dripping sweet. Y'all come to our party
>
>And we'll give you a treat. Dancing and singing around the
>
>Maypole in our orchard, don't you know.

SONG #2

Doggies

DOGGIE BOWSER

>I'm a doggie—a real bowser.
>
>You can call me by the name of Doggie Bowser.
>
>I love to party. I love to play.
>
>I'd like to do this every day.

YAPPY HOUND

>Yap, yap, yap, I love to talk.
>
>I love to talk while I walk.
>
>Talk, talk, talk, yap, yap, yap.
>
>I bet you know others just like that.

FLABBY HOUND

>Dancing lightly on my paws
>
>Is a fete for my feet.
>
>I'm a heavyweight, as you can see
>
>So there is just more of me
>
>To party.

BEES come buzzing in.

SONG #3—BEES

> Buzzin' round, buzzin' round,
>
> Off the ground, on the ground.
>
> Singing bees, stinging bees,
>
> On the leaves, in the trees.
>
> Stinging knees, zapping fleas.
>
> Honey-making bees, bees, bees.

BUBBLY BEE

> I'm a bubbly, bubbly bumble bee.
>
> But I'm not a very humble bee.
>
> I'll blow a bubble out at you,
>
> Then I'll sting you till you're purple-blue.
>
> LET'S GET *BEESY!*

DASHING BEE

> I'm making a beeline for the party. In fact, I'm dashing there.
>
> My stingers are the most beautiful,
>
> And I'll be the most dashing bee there.
>
> You will be my honey bee, won't you?

PHILOSOPHER BEE (Yiddish accent)

> To bee or not to bee. Is that a question? Such a question.
>
> If we vouldn't bee, we vouldn't am,

But since we are, we bee.

Do you understand?

GREEN APPLES

We could have been computers if we weren't so green.

But we're apples, not computers.

We'd rather be tart than smart.

(MS. AP PEL, a sexy apple, slinks and swishes into the orchard.)

APPLES (All together)

Oh my gosh! Here comes Ms. Ap pel. She's so classy. She can spell.

ORANGE JUICE (a male orange)

We have been blessed. We are the golden color of the sun.

Our sweet juices drip on everyone.

We're full of vitamin C and we're round

And appealing as we can be.

VENCIA

We grow in the orchard. We love it here, our friends are the rain and all the fresh air.

SONG #4

CHORUS

APPLES

> I'm such a happy apple
>
> I'm such a happy apple
>
> Today's a beautiful day!
>
> I've never been so excited.
>
> I'm simply delighted!

ORANGES

> We love springtime
>
> It's a sweet time.
>
> Warm beautiful
>
> Sunshine.

TOGETHER

> It's a glorious day in May.
>
> We're celebrating springtime
>
> When the sun comes shining through.
>
> We just blossom, we're so pretty
>
> And alive. And the sky's so blue.

The BEANS and PEAS enter the orchard playing jazz music. APPLES and ORANGES move aside to give the vegetables room—it is clear that the fruits don't like the Beans and Peas too much.

DITSY, a young, female bean, walks through the orchard boldly, kicking her feet in the soil, smelling the fresh morning air.

SONG #5

LOVE THE PLACE I'M IN

DITSY

    I wake up in the morning

    And I love the place I'm in.

    The beauty that surrounds me

    Astounds me.

    The freshness of the air

    And the sunshine

    Or the freely flowing rain.

    I'm so lucky to be growing

    Plainly knowing

    That I love the place I'm in.

    There's a lovely world out there.

    But I'm happy being here.

    This is my special place

    Among the human race and I hold

    It very dear.

    Being happy where I am is a

    Higher-minded plan. I will live

    With ease and grace

    Because this is my special place.

    It's so easy to survive.

    You want to be alive

When you love the place you're in.

I'm so happy to be growing

Plainly knowing

That I love the place I'm in.

PINTO (a male bean)

Somebody threw some seeds in here. Up we grew and grew and grew. We are so very happy here. We'll sway with the breezes and squeeze with the beezes.

DITSY

That's how we get full of vitamin B's.

PEAS

We're peas in a pod and we like this sod.

PIA (a female pea)

We like the orchard, even though it's not a pea's normal pad.

JONATHAN APPLESEED

Yeah, what are you doing in our place, anyway? You live in our space, and you don't belong. You belong in your own commune.

VENCIA

You belong with the vegetables, not with us fruit. You're different from us. You deserve the boot!

MR. POD (a pea)

> You shouldn't judge everything by yourselves. Others may look or seem different to you, but we can all get along if we're kind to each other and play together and work together. So let's all join in a song and dance and maybe we'll find a little romance.

The Beans and Peas attempt to dance with the apples and oranges, but the fruits back away.

ORA

> Oh, Rippley, can't we play?

VENCIA

> No way, no way! Not now or any other day!
>
> Not while those vegetables are here to stay!

VENCIA grabs the children's hands, and they leave the clearing to return to their homes in the trees. The Doggies and Bees try to get them to stay and dance with the vegetables, but to no avail.

EXTERIOR SCENE: BEAUTIFUL ORCHARD   NIGHT

Late at night, ASTRID APHID and NERDY MEDFLY arrive in the orchard.

SONG #6

WE'RE OUTRAGEOUS

ASTRID and NERDY

> We're outrageous
>
> You can't save us.

We're so nasty,

We're bombasty.

I'm Nerdy,

Down and dirty.

I'm Astrid,

I'm a real bad kid.

We cause a commotion.

What a notion.

We cause a sensation

Throughout the nation.

Being outrageous

Can be contagious.

You can't save us.

We're born to be bad.

Hee, hee, hee.

You can't catch me.

Hee, hee, hee.

You can't catch me.

You can't catch me.

ASTRID APHID

I'm a disgusting little pest.

I suck juices from green leaves.

I like beans and peas the best.

NERDY MEDFLY

I'm Nerdy Medfly. You know about me.

Apples don't want me in their family tree.

ASTRID and NERDY do a dance holding hands.

ASTRID

Let's go to their party. Let's dance up a storm.

NERDY

We'll show them who is boss. We'll do them some harm.

ASTRID

Beans and peas are good to eat.

NERDY

And apples and oranges are pretty and sweet.

ASTRID and NERDY

But we're going to get rid of them.

Who needs their vitamins anyway?

We'll take over this orchard without delay.

All the orchards will be ours one day.

We'll rule the orchards like a king and queen.

And we'll be ugly and real mean.

EXTERIOR SCENE: TREE HOUSES   BEAUTIFUL ORCHARD   DAY

    The apples, oranges, doggies and bees are preparing for the party.

DOGGIE BOWSER

    I'm glad you let me help you bake.

    Mmmm. I love a chocolate cake.

APPLE-ACIA

    We need your help. We're glad you're here.

    This is the biggest party of the year.

SWEET APPLE

    Bubbly Bee, take this spoon to Miss Orange, will you please?

    You know, she really loves you bees.

MS. APPEL talking to PHILOSOPHER BEE

    Philosopher Bee, why in the world do those beans and peas

    Have to grow under our very own trees?

    They are so ghastly long and green.

    They are the ugliest things I've even seen.

MS. AP PEL looks down through the tree limbs, sees the beans and peas jamming on musical instruments on the orchard floor.

ORANGE JUICE (male orange)

    The music they play is terrible, too.

    It's different from any music I ever knew.

We apples and oranges grew up with class.

Our parents never played that awful jazz.

VENCIA

They disgust me. They really do.

They should be red or orange. Their color won't do.

PHILOSOPHER BEE

Vencia, Vencia, listen to you.

Beans and peas are nice—and worthy, too.

Remember, when you were young,

You had a greenish hue.

SWEET APPLE

The doggies and bees are such good guests.

They are so cute. They look their best.

Those darn beans and peas want to play with us too.

I wish we could get rid of them, oh poo!

They grow in our orchard, and I don't know why.

VENCIA

They're not like us at all.

I don't like them. I can't even try.

SONG #7

AIN'T NO ROOM FOR BEANS AND PEAS

VENCIA

We're blessed with our land.

This should just be our land.

This space was meant

For you and me.

We're very special.

We have no equal.

We're so pretty, so pretty!

There's just no room here

For the beans and peas.

There ain't no room for the beans and peas.

They're so ugly they make me sneeze.

We're all so pretty, orange and red.

They're just plain green.

They shouldn't be seen.

Well, I mean.

(Well, she means)

(Well, we mean)

There just ain't no room here for the beans and peas.

Leave us.

Leave us alone.

This is our place.

It should be our own!

YAPPY HOUND

Let's all be friends. We can get along.

You're picking on them and you're totally wrong.

DASHING BEE

They're really good guys.

You're not giving them a chance.

They don't deserve your nasty glance.

PHILOSOPHER BEE

What did they do to you anyway?

Why do you hate them? What did they say?

RIPPLEY and ORA come skipping up to APPLE-ACIA.

RIPPLEY

Bye, Mom. We're going off to play.

We're going to have some fun today.

APPLE-ACIA

Yes, you may go out that way.

But we don't want you and the beans and peas to play.

RIPPLEY

Yes, we know what you mean. We won't play with them. We're just as good as they are.

ORA

> We don't like their color green.

EXTERIOR SCENE: BEAUTIFUL ORCHARD   DAY

RIPPLEY and ORA chase each other through the orchard, laughing. RIPPLEY stops short, spies the young beans and peas playing on tall, green stilts.

RIPPLEY

> Oh,, look over there. Are they playing a game?

ORA

> Let's sneak up and see. What's it called? What could it be?

YOUNG BEANS and PEAS see them.

DITSY

> Come join us. We're having fun.
>
> Come on. This game is for anyone.

RIPPLEY and ORA

> We're not supposed to play with you.

HUNKY (young, male pea)

> Why not? We're your neighbors too.

RIPPLEY (to ORA)

    Let's play. What can it hurt? They're playing Jack and the Beanstalk.

RIPPLEY and ORA run to the vegetables, join in their fun. FLABBY HOUND saunters by, balancing a giant bone on his nose. He hears the children playing, turns to take a look. FLABBY HOUND is shocked to see the young apples and oranges playing with the young beans and peas. FLABBY HOUND sneaks off quietly.

EXTERIOR SCENE: BEAUTIFUL ORCHARD   DAY

FLABBY HOUND approaches his friends, the bees, who are busy preparing honey.

FLABBY HOUND

    Guess what I saw. It was new to me.

    I saw a young apple and orange playing with a young bean and pea.

PHILOSOPHER BEE

    Oh, oh. Ms. APPLE and Ms. VENCIA don't want them to.

    They would certainly punish them if they knew. Oy!

YAPPY HOUND'S ears perk up behind them.

EXTERIOR SCENE: BEAUTIFUL ORCHARD   DAY

APPLES and ORANGES are preparing for the party in their own camp. Beans and Peas are doing the same on their side of the camp. Beans and Peas are talking to themselves.

27

HUNKY AND DITSY

    Mom, Dad, tell us why the big apples and oranges don't like us.

SONG #8

SNOOTY FRUITY

MOM and DAD BEANS and PEAS

    They think they're very pretty.

    They think they're simply swell.

    Our color doesn't suit them.

    They say we're very dull.

    They've got an affectation.

    They're snooty little fruit.

    They think we're not bright.

    Our color doesn't suit!

    But little ones,

    Precious little ones.

    Even if we're dull and plain

    We're just as good as they are

    So you see, kids, we're just the same!

ON THE APPLE AND ORANGE SIDE (STAGE RIGHT)

YAPPY HOUND

> Yap, yap, yap. Your kids are so cute. Playing on the beanstalk.
>
> Oh, I'd better be mute. (He covers his mouth with his hands).

APPLE-ACIA gasps. VENCIA fumes. They call in the children.

APPLES and ORANGES

> Kids, kids, come in now!
>
> We're upset with you and HOW!

ORA and RIPPLEY come running in.

APPLE-ACIA

> Why were you playing with the peas and beans?

RIPPLEY

> Because we like them. They're fun and not mean.

VENCIA

> Well, you're naughty, naughty, naughty
>
> And we'll just see
>
> If you'll be playing with the beans and peas.

They strut across stage to talk to parent beans and parent peas, but before they arrive, ASTRID and NERDY dash onto the stage, crashing their party.

The oranges and apples turn to the doggies and bees, frightened.

SONG #9

WE'RE AS NASTY AS CAN BE

ASTRID and NERDY

> Ho, ho, ho. Hee, hee, hee.
>
> We're as nasty as we can be.
>
> We're going to squish you
>
> We're going to squash you
>
> We're going to eat you with glee.
>
> You'll all look so good in our tummy.
>
> Hey, hey! What you say?
>
> Hey, hey! What you say?
>
> You are going to make our day!
>
> What you say?

APPLES and ORANGES, BEANS and PEAS

> Oh my gosh, hisses, those awful creatures are here.
>
> They'll destroy our bodies and we'll look real weird.

APPLES and ORANGES

> Let's figure a way to stop them soon.

Before our crops get a healthy bloom.

JONATHAN APPLESEED

Let's scrape them and scratch them and squirt them with glee (takes a hose).

Yuck, I don't want them even close to me.

ORANGE JUICE

Let's push them and shove them and stomp on them too.

Those awful bugs will make a real good goo.

APPLES

Let's get some poison. We'll get rid of these fiends.

BEANS

Yeh, let's do it before they bake our beans.

APPLES and ORANGES, BEANS and PEAS

They want to take over this orchard. Of that we're quite clear. Let's get the poison pellets.

ORANGES

They're over here!

EXTERIOR SCENE: ORCHARD   DAY

RIPPLEY and ORA are alone.

RIPPLEY

Gosh, I heard Mom and Dad plan to poison the aphids and medfly. That gives me quite a scare. What if they ruin the whole orchard with poison?

ORA

And it becomes totally bare!

HUNKY and DITSY sneak in to see them. RIPPLEY and ORA laugh, genuinely happy to see them.

HUNKY

We're sorry you got in trouble. What can we do for you?

RIPPLEY

You can help us figure out how to get rid of the awful Aphid and that Nerdy Medfly.

ORA

It's not right to poison them.

RIPPLEY

It could affect the entire orchard, and that means
You and us
And our moms and dads
And the Bees and the Doggies.

The beans and peas confer among themselves.

DITSY

Mmm, mmm. We have an idea. Now listen to this.

We've got a plan that simply can't miss.

Let's go to the garden—the flowers will help.

DITSY

They'll give us some petals, some sweet pleasant petals, and soon we'll have nothing to fear.

HUNKY

Astrid the Aphid won't be awful anymore and the petals will take the meddle out of the medfly. You'll see, they will be as nice as can be.

EXTERIOR SCENE: FLOWER GARDEN   DAY

ORA, RIPPLEY, DITSY and HUNKY crawl through the foliage and emerge in a mystical flower garden.

The flowers are swaying and singing.

SONG #10

PERFUME

FLOWER

    Perfume.

    Surround your senses with the perfume

    Of our blossoms.

    Nurture your soul with the sweet scent,

    Sent from the heavens.

    This is the essence of us.

    Our perfumed petals

Will envelope your being.

Lifting you gently to a higher plane.

Awakening

Pulsating

Your brain.

A gentle breeze will carry off our talents

And a marinating balance

Will seep into your worlds again.

Perfume.

Surround your senses with the perfume of

Our blossoms.

Nurture your soul with the sweet scent

Sent from the heavens.

This is the essence of us.

OTHER FLOWERS

Breathing in our magic presence

Will stimulate the senses

And bring peace into your lives again.

ORA

Hi, hi you beautiful sweet things.

You look so pretty and you smell so good.

No wonder you're always in such a good mood.

FLOWER

> Yes, we are always pleasant. We don't have attitudes.
>
> We bring love and happiness and light into lives.
>
> If you are a little unhappy and feel some gloom
>
> Just bend over and smell our perfume.

APPLE AND ORANGE, BEANS AND PEAS

> Yes, yes—that's why we're here.
>
> You must save us, you must help us, oh dear!

FLOWER

> What can we do?
>
> What in the world is troubling you?

HUNKY

> Our orchard will be poisoned and we'll surely all die.
>
> We must have your pleasant petals for the Aphid and Medfly.

ORA

> We want to change those nasty creatures and make them pleasant like us.

RIPPLEY

> They want to take over our orchard and become king and queen.
>
> Don't you think they're awfully mean?

FLOWER

>Yes, yes we do!

>Take our petals. We'll help you.

They all start gathering petals.

EXTERIOR SCENE: BEAUTIFUL ORCHARD   DAY

ASTRID APHID and NERDY MEDFLY prepare dynamite to destroy the oranges, apples, beans and peas.

ASTRID and NERDY

>Hey, we'll get them. We'll blow them up now.

>We want to take over the orchards so we'll give them a *POW*.

ASTRID

>Hey, big fella. What do you say?

>You know we'll rule here one day.

NERDY

>Well, of course we will.

>This orchard is OURS. Make no mistake.

>This is just a piece of cake.

ASTRID (struts around)

>We'll be so powerful

>All this will be ours.

>We'll have all this land

And the biggest house.

Maybe we'll make them bow down to us.

We'll put them in their place.

NERDY

Yeh. They're going to go to waste.

BOTH

Ha, ha, ha.

Meanwhile Apples, Oranges, Beans and Peas sneak up dragging an old cannon behind them. They lift a grapefruit-sized poison pellet and load it into the cannon barrel.

JONATHAN APPLESEED

These poison pellets will take care of those awful bugs

They're acting like a couple of thugs.

PIA

This will kill them and we'll be free.

Then we can live again peacefully.

Suddenly a cloud of flower petals begins to fall from the sky.

BEANS and PEAS

Wait, look around

Look what's falling to the ground.

BEANS, PEAS, APPLES and ORANGES

>They're pleasant petals. We can tell.

>They're heaven sent. Such a pleasant smell!

ORA, RIPPLEY, HUNKY and DITSY

>It's us, it's us. We're throwing them down.

>We're scattering them all around.

RIPPLEY

>We don't need your poison

>These will work instead.

HUNKY

>Perfumed petals change bugs

>Without making them dead.

ASTRID and NERDY stop lighting their dynamite. They stagger, looking goofy.

ASTRID

>Our friends are here—these nice vegetables.

>And all these good fruits.

>And our friends, the doggies and bees.

NERDY

>We should all be dancing, shouldn't we?

>This is your orchard. We want to work with you.

>We want you healthy, we certainly do!

MEDFLY and APHID walk, dance like moonwalkers to rap song.

SONG #11

WE FEEL REAL GOOD

MEDFLY and APHID

        We feel real good

        We feel real kind.

        These are all our friends

        We must have been blind.

        We're not going to make trouble

        Not anymore.

        We'll all live together.

        Let's even the score.

        We were put on this earth

        For some reason, we know.

        We're going to work together

        So we all can grow.

JONATHAN APPLESEED

        Our children saved the day.

        They showed us the better way.

SWEET APPLE

        It started when the young ones went out to play.

SONG #12

YOUTH

EVERYONE

Youth!

Wonderful youth!

They see what is right.

They see the truth.

Their days are not gloomy

Even when it's not sunny.

Their world is great fun.

They see good in everyone.

So listen to your children,

Heed what they have to say.

Their innocence is beautiful

It may be the better way.

CHILDREN

We're awfully bubbly.

Sometimes we're troublely.

La la la la.

We try to do our best

But we're often just a pest.

We're brave and smart

We're also clever.

We do our part.

To make things better!

APPLE-ACIA (to BEANS and PEAS)

You are our friends. We can all live together. We'll make amends.

STRINGY (a male bean)

We're not so different. We see that now. We're all related anyhow.

APPLES and ORANGES run to BEANS and PEAS.

VENCIA is still reluctant.

ORA

Come on, Vencia!

DITSY pulls out her saxophone.

DITSY

I'll play some music for you.

DITSY plays some jazz, hoping to lure VENCIA to their side. VENCIA at first appears even more angered by the music, but suddenly a shower of flower petals falls close around her head.

We see RIPPLEY in the trees above her, pouring a bucket full of petals. He gives the "thumbs up" sign to DITSY.

VENCIA changes her tune.

VENCIA

Oh, I LOVE that music!

She runs over to join the rest of the fruits and vegetables.

APPLES and ORANGES

This orchard is big enough for all of us. Oh my gosh—swoosh! Let's be friends. Let's live in Harmony!

BEANS and PEAS shake their hands

Yes, yes. Our buddies, our buddies

APPLES and ORANGES, BEANS, PEAS, DOGGIES, BEES, MEDFLY and APHID

For the good of us all and for all our friends

We joined together and made amends.

We can live side by side on the earth, in the rain and the sun

VENCIA

And we don't have to be mad at anyone.

We're in a state of perfect HARMONY.

FINAL SONG #13

PERFECT HARMONY

EVERYONE

Harmony

A little taking here.
A little giving there.
Sharing, caring, being aware.

We know you're sometimes lazy.
You're sometimes too slow.
Well, We know you can be silly
And at night you always snore.

But we'll over look these problems
And love you even more.

Sometimes you act so stupid
Sometimes you dress too bright.
You often are so jealous,
And wear your clothes too tight.

You get yourself so dirty
When you're rolling on the ground.
You get so stiff and angry
And make a funny sound.

But we'll over look these differences
They will not bother us

This is a beautiful day.
We've found a peaceful way
To live together
In good or bad weather.
We'll work as a team
Building our dream.
What a pleasant scene.

We're as happy as can be!
We're going to live in ...

Harmony!

THIS IS HARMONY!

THE END